# Old MILNGAVIE

*by*
## James Crawford

© James Crawford 1996
First published in the United Kingdom, 1996
by StenlakePublishing
Telephone/Fax: 01290 551122

ISBN 1 872074 86 3

PIC-NICS AT MILNGAVIE RESERVOIR
WAITING TILL THE CLOUDS ROLL BY

The Mugdock and Craigmaddie reservoirs were popular with Glasgow residents who came to Milngavie by train and walked to the attractive gardens, maintained by the Corporation Waterworks, for their picnics. Unfortunately one could not always rely on the weather. Who says everything was better in the old days! This postcard dates from *c.*1910.

# Acknowledgements

I would like to thank all my friends who encouraged me to
compile this book, and my wife who coped with translating
my garbled longhand notes into intelligible typed script.

IN MILNGAVIE

*This place is noted for its Waterworks – Two large lochs which supply the water to Glasgow. It originally comes from Loch Katrine. "Milngavie" is pronounced "Mulguy = Mae"*

Main Street looking south towards Glasgow, 1902. This postcard dates from the era when only the name and address of the recipient could be written on the reverse, and a small picture was printed on the front leaving space for the message next to it. In addition to a brief description of Milngavie the writer has provided details of how to pronounce its name. Enough said!

*West End, Milngavie.*

RELIABLE SERIES.

The horse bus for Balfron, photographed *c*.1880. Rob Roy is reputed to have frequented the Douglas Arms. Its proprietor when this picture was taken was Charles Bissland. He was the first honorary treasurer of the Burgh of Milngavie, which was formed in 1875 when its population was 2,184. The car park and Royal Bank of Scotland in Douglas Street now occupy this site.

THE "ALLANDER" AT ENTRANCE TO PUBLIC PARK, MILNGAVIE.

Gavins Mill with the footbridge from Main Street to the park in the background, photographed in 1905.  A mill has stood on this site for many centuries, and one of the oldest historical sources states that by the reign of James IV (1488-1513) it had already 'long been in use'.  Milngavie grew round the mill, which remained in operation into the twentieth century, when it was allowed to fall into disrepair.  In the 1960s it was refurbished and converted into architects' offices and a tearoom, with the original waterwheel retained as a feature.  It is now an Indian restaurant and a category 'B' listed building.

The origin of the name Milngavie (pronounced 'Millguy') is uncertain, although it is probably connected to this meal or grain mill. Local tradition claims that it was built for the Dukes of Montrose by one named Guy giving – hey presto – 'Mill O Guy', a plausible explanation. The name 'Milgay' appears on Timothy Pont's 1654 map of The Lennox, which was published in Blaeu's Atlas.

Main Street, 1909. The Black Bull, on the left, can trace its history back to 1827 and is the oldest hostelry in the town. Milngavie's first post office occupied a building that adjoins the Black Bull but predates it by ten years. Many changes have taken place to the buildings on the left since this picture was taken.

Main Street looking towards the Douglas Arms during the late nineteenth century, with some outside staircases still in evidence. In the late 1800s, most of the street's residents were employed at the Turkey Red works at Burnbrae and when they left for work early in the morning, the noise of their clogs on the cobble stones is said to have made quite a cacophony. The building on the left was demolished in the 1920s to make way for the Douglas Cinema, while the fountain on the right remained *in situ* until Woodburn Way was built in the early 1970s.

Douglas Street photographed from the end of Main Street, looking towards the Cross Keys Inn and Station Road. Mr McIntosh the policeman is crossing the street. Note the interesting chimney with the 'granny' on it, on the roof above Coia's Emporium. The horse and cart belongs to Baird the Glasgow carrier, and has just been passed by a Watt Brothers bus.

Milngavie's War Memorial was unveiled by Brigadier General Campbell Douglas CB on Sunday 17 September 1922. It was erected in the Douglas Park Gardens, previously the site of the Milngavie Gas Works. Milngavie's first Parish Church can be seen in the background of this picture.

CHEAPSIDE STREET, MILNGAVIE. №645/20 RELIABLE SERIES

Mugdock Road was called Cheapside Street when this turn of the century picture was taken. I have not been able to discover why so many children are gathered in this picture, although in the early days of photography it was common for a camera to draw a crowd. The Cross Keys Inn is visible on the right, with a fruit shop and a branch of the Royal Bank across the road from it. At one time Milngavie was a market town, and an annual fair was held near the Cross Keys for the sale of cattle – not to mention the exchange of wives – or so legend would have us believe. Fairs ceased after 1830, due to the outbreak of cholera in Scotland and the corresponding threat of infection.

A later view of Cheapside with the Royal Bank on the left, and a bus approaching from Mugdockbank in the distance. With the exception of the building on the immediate right – the Cross Keys Inn – all of the properties on this side of the street have been demolished. There were around twelve public houses in Milngavie at the turn of the century, which for a town of its size seems a lot. It's a shame we can't still park outside shops without worrying about yellow lines.

Cairns U.F. Church, Milngavie

When this picture was taken *c*.1904, Cairns Church, its manse (to the left) and hall (behind the church) had only recently been completed. The opening service was held on the evening of Friday 8 May 1903 when the Rev. Professor Hislop DD preached to a sizeable congregation. The collection amounted to the tidy sum of £31. Previously the congregation had held its services in the church in Kirk Street (now Mugdock Road), situated on the edge of Barloch Moor and shown opposite. The new church took its name from Professor John Cairns, principal of the United Presbyterian Hall from 1879 to 1892.

Kirk Street (now part of Mugdock Road) looking north towards Mugdock and Strathblane. The substantial building on the right was the first church in the 'village'. It was completed in 1799 at a cost of nearly £500, and led to the name Kirk Street. By the time this picture was taken in 1900 there was considerable decay in the roof and the church required extensive repairs. A site for a new building was secured on Dougalston Estate and church, hall and manse were subsequently built there at a cost of £8,000. In this picture, Simpson's Tea Rooms occupy the two storey building at the extreme left.

Dr Thomas Chalmers, the great Scottish church leader, was responsible for the establishment of Milngavie Parish Church which was built at a cost of £1,500 and opened in 1840.  He visited the village in the late 1830s and found that 'souls were perishing for lack of sustenance'.  By 1904 the church was not big enough for its congregation and a new site was acquired for the building of St Pauls, which opened in 1906.  The old Parish Church still stands, having been used for Civil Defence and as temporary accommodation after the town hall burnt down in 1940.  It has now been converted into flats.

Douglas Street looking towards the Cross Keys Inn and the old Parish Church, 1909. The Douglas Arms is just out of picture to the left. Nowadays Iceland, MacDonald Eadie and other new shops occupy this site, with Copland & Lye's clock in the immediate foreground and the war memorial on the right.

This picture of the Glasgow Corporation Waterworks at Milngavie, dating from about 1904, shows the well kept gardens and greenhouse which were open to the public. The monument to James Morris Gale, M.Inst CE, is visible to the left. Gale was the chief engineer at the waterworks, and designed the entire water system from Loch Katrine to Milngavie – in addition to carrying out his normal maintenance duties and supervising the engineering staff under his control.

Glasgow Corporation's new petrol motor fire pumps at Mugdock Reservoir, 1907. Parts of Glasgow where there were many mills and warehouses had a sophisticated system of pipes and firecocks which the steam fire engines could easily attach up to. However, many of the outlying districts were entirely without any form of fire extinguishing facilities, hence the importance of these new engines.

Tannoch Loch photographed from the top of the reservoir bank prior to 1900. The loch is artificial, and was previously a marshy football field which extended in one direction from the vicinity of Tannoch Drive to the bank of Mugdock Reservoir, and in the other from Mugdock Road to Heathfield Drive. Around 1895 the area was acquired by the builder John Woodburn, who dammed the Tannoch Burn which ran alongside Heathfield Drive. The purpose was to create a hydro-electric plant, providing power to light Clober Crescent in Station Road.

Milngavie from the Water Works.

Tannoch Loch, looking across to Montrose Gardens, photographed from the top of Mugdock Road. The roof of the house in the foreground is the last villa in Heathfield Drive. This picture was taken about thirty years later than the one opposite, and it is gratifying to see how much the trees have grown. The chimney on the horizon belonged to the paper mill.

BUCHANAN STREET, MILNGAVIE

D 2540

Buchanan Street looking north towards Cairns Church and the junction with Cairns Drive. Note the gas street lamps, still present in the late fifties. It was only in the late twenties that Buchanan Street was extended from Cairns Church to connect with Tannoch Drive, Heathfield Drive and Craigmillar Avenue.

Tannoch Loch and Heathfield Drive, 1903. John Woodburn, a former provost of the burgh, tipped soil and stones along the line of what is now Tannoch Drive to form an embankment and create Tannoch Loch. Once the embankment was high enough two overflows were created, one just west of Heathfield Drive and the other east of 9 Tannoch Drive. The run-off from these forms Tannoch Burn, which meanders across Barloch Moor to the River Allander. Woodburn installed a scour pipe between these overflows to feed his small hydro-electric plant, and a pier was built over the pipe to provide access to its valve. However, Woodburn did not take any precautions to prevent consolidation or water filtering through the embankment, and over the years various subsidences have occurred. In 1935 a concrete raft had to be constructed under the part of Tannoch Drive which borders the loch to counteract the problem.

Station Road, Milngavie.

Milngavie's main street has always been better known as Station Road. This picture, looking east, was taken *c*.1925 from the bridge over the branch line to the paper mill. Cheapside (or Mugdock Road as it is now known) and the Cross Keys Inn are on the left. The cupola on the building to the right has, sadly, long since been removed. This belongs to the property which Woodburn proposed to illuminate with electricity generated from his hydro-electric scheme, and the inscription below the dome reads 'Clober Crescent'.

STATION ROAD FROM CROSS KEYS, MILNGAVIE

Forty years on and not much has changed, except that the cupola has been removed and the ground floor of the corner building has become a branch of the Bank of Scotland. With the increase in traffic, there is now a Belisha crossing outside the Cross Keys Inn, at the entrance to Mugdock Road. The shadows suggest that this picture was taken early in the morning before the shops opened.

Station Road looking west, c.1904. Today the street is pedestrianised, and the single storey property on the right (more clearly visible in the picture opposite) has been demolished. The building to the left of it with the white frontage was removed in the 1970s to make way for the Co-op which now occupies the spot. Again, I don't know why the crowds of school children have gathered in the street. Their segregation, with boys on the left and girls on the right, is reminiscent of school dance classes!

A close-up of some of the shops on the north side of Station Road, c.1900. Weir's grocers served as the local post office, and the staff standing outside the shop are wearing post office uniforms. The Weir family ran the post office for some thirty years. In the 1880s the mail arrived from Glasgow around 3.00 a.m. Rumour has it that rather than getting up and going downstairs to deal with the mails, the Weirs would just open the window to lower the outgoing mail on a rope and haul up the deliveries. Most of this row of shops has now been demolished. Wm McMillan's jewellers was removed to give access to the service road running parallel to the street, while the building that accommodated the grocers and saddlers has made way for a new Co-op.

Milngavie Railway Station prior to electrification in 1961. The line was opened in 1863 and a second set of tracks was laid under the 1897 North British Railway General Powers Act.  Part of the branch line to the Ellangowan Paper Mill, visible to the left, now forms the road off Woodburn Way.  This passes under Milngavie's pedestrianised area and becomes Mugdock Road just beyond the Red Cross car park.

The entrance to Milngavie Goods Yard, which was closed in the late sixties and is now a light industrial estate and car park. Crossveggate Farm, which has been replaced by housing, is visible in the background.

This attractive terrace of eight houses, named Southview, overlooked the station and public park. It was demolished to make way for Woodburn Way, Milngavie's bypass, as part of the town's pedestrianisation programme. This picture was taken in 1910 and shows the steeple of the old Parish Church in the background.

The station complex photographed from the bridge between Crossveggate Farm and the public park, 1909. The goods yard lies to the right of the station, with the branch line to Ellangowan Paper Mill to the left of it. Southview Terrace is visible on the far left, with the back of Station Road and the Old Parish Church steeple on the horizon. The substantial stone building in the background is Milngavie Primary School, and this distant shot is the only postcard view I have seen of it. Cairns Church stands on the right of the picture, with the UF Church (now St Joseph's) in front of it and the houses of Grange Avenue to the left. Notice how busy the goods yard looks. It's a pity we can't get the 'goods' back on to the railway to save our streets!

The junction of Station Road, Strathblane Road, Baldernock Road and Glasgow Road, *c*.1900. The building on the immediate left was occupied by the McAulay family for over one hundred years, hence the local name McAulay's Corner. James McAulay, the burgh's third Provost, was born here in 1834 and was still a resident when he died in 1925. The whitewashed cottages on the other side of the junction were occupied by workers on the Dougalston Estate. In 1905, the owner of the estate, J.R. Ker, gifted this area for the building of the new Parish Church (named St Paul's under the 1929 Act of Union). The Allander Public House now stands on the corner occupied by the Newtown Vaults. Victoria Place, which occupies the fourth corner, dated from 1883 and was home to David Hunter's Provision Merchant's at one time. Along with the adjoining tenements on Glasgow Road and Station Road, the shop was demolished sometime ago to be replaced by a modern housing estate, wherein the name Victoria Place survives.

Station Road looking towards Garwhitter Brae (now Baldernock Road) and Strathblane Road. The gate leading to Milngavie and Bearsden UF Church is on the immediate left of this 1909 photograph. It later became St Luke's Church of Scotland, and more recently St Joseph's RC Church. The present town hall and Lillie Art Gallery stand on the site of the burgh hall (on the left), which burnt down on 22 April 1940. The police station stood just beyond the burgh hall.

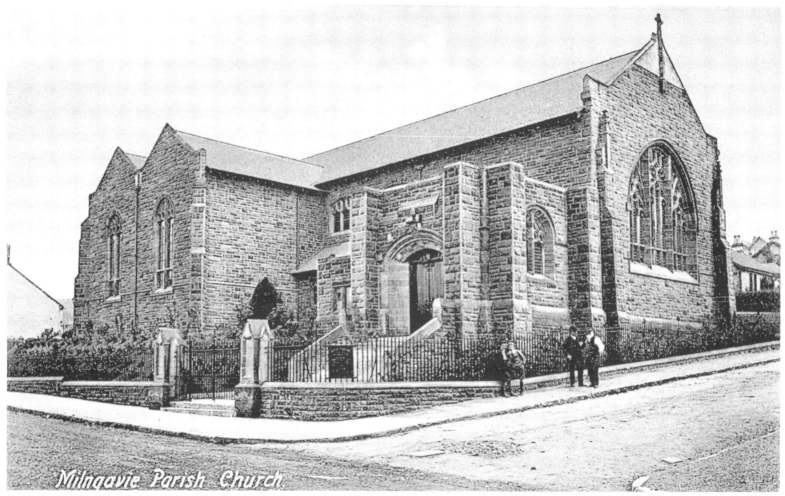

Milngavie Parish Church.

In 1840 the Presbytery of Dumbarton and the Kirk Session of New Kilpatrick took steps to build a parish church in Milngavie. The building was completed in 1841 but with membership reaching 700 larger premises were required by 1904. A site in the new town at the foot of Garwhitter Brae was gifted by J. Ripley Ker of Douglaston, and the competition to design the new church was won by Messrs Leadbetter and Fairley of Edinburgh. The memorial stone was laid by Her Grace the Duchess of Montrose on Saturday 20 May 1905 and the new Parish Church was dedicated on Friday 12 January 1906. This picture was taken soon afterwards.

Station Road photographed from the roof of St Paul's Church during the late thirties. Victoria Place is on the left and McAulay Corner to the right. By this time the 'McAulay Cottage' had been demolished and replaced by a detached villa alongside tenements. The villa and McLay's garage behind it have also since gone, to be replaced in turn by Holmbrae House.

Strathblane Road, Milngavie

Strathblane Road, with Station Road on the left and St Paul's Church and Baldernock Road to the right. At the entrance to the church a lamplighter is visible on his ladder. Both gas lamps and telegraph poles have now been removed, and today the telephone cables are underground. Most of the buildings on the left are still standing, but apart from the church none of the ones on the right have survived. This picture was taken during the early 1930s. The metal railings around the church were subsequently removed for the war effort.

Strathblane Road during the thirties again, with Kersland Lane on the left. A modern block of flats and a small industrial estate have replaced the buildings to the right.

Ladywood, Milngavie

Ladywood was occupied by the Sisters of Notre Dame until it was sold for a housing development in the 1970s. Flats, also called Ladywood, now occupy the site. With its conservatory and creepers on the walls, this 1910 view of the house looks similar to many of the detached villas in the area today.

MILNGAVIE WAR WEAPONS WEEK 6/9/41 8.

Like other communities, Milngavie held annual War Weapons Weeks during the Second World War to raise funds through the sale of war savings certificates. The County of Dunbarton's War Weapons Week for 1941 was held from 6 to 13 September and aimed to raise £350,000. However, after five days the magnificent sum of £492,812 had been collected. *'The object of this effort is to ensure that every available amount is brought forth from current accounts, money boxes and monies kept in the homes of the people and put at the disposal of the government to aid the great war effort.'* *'This is the time to make a real sacrifice on behalf of your country. He who only gives what he can afford, gives nothing.'* Stirring words indeed. This picture shows part of the procession of military, civil defence and voluntary services marching down Strathblane Road. Note the tape over the windows on the left hand side of the street, put up to protect the glass from bomb blasts.

Baldernock Free Church stood in the grounds of Baldernock House, and with its earth floor must have been very Spartan. A sizeable portion of the church's congregation came from Milngavie, and in 1896 the church moved there. However, the new Baldernock and Milngavie United Free Church subsequently became the UF Church, then in 1929 St Luke's and latterly St Joseph's Roman Catholic Church. The original building, seen here around 1907, was acquired by Baldernock House and converted into a garage. Both buildings have had chequered careers.

Baldernock Parish Church has a long history, with parish records dating from 1690. In 1575 the Rev. John Anderson was the first post-Reformation minister to be appointed to Kilpatrick Parish. He had a 'reader' appointed for Baldernock which suggests that it is probably a pre Reformation church. In the era of bodysnatchers, church officials used the small stone building at the entrance to the graveyard to guard the newly interred from their attention. The present building was constructed in 1795 at a cost of £435 17s 5d. This photograph dates from the 1930s.

An unusual view of Craigmaddie House, which was used as a convalescent home for injured soldiers during the First World War. The postcard was sent by one 'JB', who was probably convalescing at Craigmaddie. It is addressed to a Private Rodger of the Argyll and Sutherland Highlanders at Dreghorn Barracks, Colinton, Edinburgh. He seems to have spent time at Craigmaddie too for the message reads *'Just a reminder from Milguy. We have had good weather which makes it all the more enjoyable. Hoping you are keeping healthy and strong.'* Craigmaddie is currently owned by the Struthers family, and previously belonged to Robert Ker who acquired it and Douglaston in 1870.

The Auld Wives' Lifts are situated on the moor to the east of Craigmaddie House. The meaning of the name Craigmaddie is 'Rock of God' and the lifts consist of two massive prismatic shaped stones alongside each other, with a third stone, eighteen feet long, lying across them so as to form a sort of altar. The origins of the Lifts rest in the mists of time, but could be druidical. A circle of oak trees stood nearby until the middle of the nineteenth century, giving credence to this theory. However, I prefer the legend which claims that three women from Campsie, Strathblane and Baldernock tried their strength by placing the stones in position. These well dressed gentlemen give an excellent idea of the size of the Lifts.

Bearsden and Milngavie Historical Society has been able to trace over one hundred farms in the district from old maps, session records and valuation rolls. The first farm machinery to appear in the area arrived in the late nineteenth century, and took the form of binders to cut and tie grain into sheaves. As this picture dates from *c.*1904, this was perhaps the first such machine. Bardowie Loch and Castle (which dates back to at least 1550) is visible in the background.

Allander Toll, Milngavie.

Nowadays Allander Toll is the site of the roundabout on the Auchenhowie Road where roads from Balmore, Bearsden and Milngavie meet. Until the middle of the nineteenth century turnpike trustees charged for passage along their stretch of road. These charges were made to assist with the cost of maintaining the roads, although at the end of the day the trustees were personally liable for keeping them in a usable state. Tolls were being charged as late as 1883 when the responsibility of maintaining roads passed to the local authority. Monies were collected not only at Allander but also at Canniesburn.

MILNGAVIE FROM GLASGOW ROAD.

216050. J.V.

A 1932 picture of Milngavie taken from what is now the approximate site of Mosshead Road, Bearsden. The Bennie Railplane can be made out just above the front of the bus, with the supports for its track extending to the right. By this time tram tracks had been laid in Glasgow Road, but agreement had not been reached with the railway company to allow the trams to cross the railway bridge at Hillfoot.

5780.

George Bennie's railplane was a revolutionary form of propellor-driven transport which combined the features of an aeroplane and a railway and was equipped with luxurious carriages capable of carrying fifty passengers. The design was intended to complement, not replace the railways, carrying passengers and mail while heavy goods would continue to use the trains below. As it ran on a suspended structure the building costs would have been lower than for normal rail track, with the need for bridges and tunnels largely avoided. Bennie calculated that the railplane could achieve speeds of 120 mph, but due to the limited length of track, a maximum of only 50 mph was reached in 1931. However, the project was too revolutionary for its time and by 1933 the trials had ceased. The structure and carriage remained as a monument to their inventor's vision until they were scrapped in 1956.

Despite its neighbour, Glasgow, having the second largest tram network in Britain, it took almost thirty years for trams to reach Milngavie. Plebiscites were held in 1907 and 1913 regarding extension of the line from Killermont to the burgh, and although the vote was in favour both times, various delays meant that there was no service until 1934. In October that year service No.13 left Milngavie for Mount Florida, and a few days later a further route (No.14) to Renfrew Ferry was started. At 22 ¾ miles it must have been quite a journey, travelling through Glasgow to Shawlands, Barrhead, Paisley and on to the Renfrew Ferry, and all for tuppence ha'penny. After the war trams were available to Broomhouse and to Gairbraid Avenue. However by the mid-fifties the day of the tram was coming to a close, and the last car from Milngavie to Maryhill travelled on 3 November 1956. The local terminus, above, was in Main Street at the junction with Park Road.

Main Street, 1957. The building in the distance, once the Douglas Arms, is occupied by a branch of the Commercial Bank of Scotland in this picture. In 1971 this was demolished to make way for The Royal Bank and Wm Low's supermarket, now Iceland. An extension to the Black Bull and the row of shops 'underneath the arches' now occupy the right hand side of the picture. Following the success of cinema screenings in the burgh hall, the Breckenridge Family built the Douglas Cinema, on the left, in 1927. However, with the advent of television and decline in the popularity of cinemas, the property was acquired by Cochranes the grocers who operated it as a early supermarket for a number of years. The building still stands and perhaps its use has gone full circle as now one of the occupants is a video hire firm.

West of Scotland Laundry, Milngavie.

645/62

The 'old laundry', as it was called, was started in 1882 by Robert Learmont and Joseph K. Fairlie on a site now occupied by the Scout Hall in Main Street. However, the business soon outgrew its premises and new ones were built in Clober Road at the junction with Craigton Road, with the most up-to-date machinery for the processing of linen installed. In fact, the West of Scotland Laundry was considered to be one of the best equipped in Scotland, and with staff numbering over two hundred at one time was one of the main employers in the town. After the 1939-45 war, and with the advent of washing machines, the business closed. A block of flats occupies the site now. In this picture the chimney and other buildings are visible beyond the Allander. The branch line and the pond belonging to the paper mill are in the foreground. Part of the pond survives today by the Community Education Centre and Library.

CLOBER ROAD, MILNGAVIE.

The view down Clober Road looking towards what is now the industrial estate, 1904, with the chimney belonging to the West of Scotland Laundry on the right. Established in 1882, the laundry was responsible for the residential development in Clober Road visible here. The driver of the pony and trap in the foreground of this picture is believed to be Mr Adam, manager of the Milngavie Gas Works. Just behind him is the bridge over the Craigton Burn, which was culverted when Balvie Road was built in the 1920s. I have another postcard, dating from 1905, showing the fronts of the houses at the far end of Clober Road with cows grazing on the field between the Allander and the road.

Clober House was situated near the junction of Birrell Road, Blackwood Road and McGrigor Road, and families of these names all had associations with it. The original property was built by James McGrigor, a Glasgow merchant and one-time owner of the Cloberfield Bleachfield works. His son-in-law, the well known Greenock engineer James Watt, designed the bleachfields. In 1912 the Duke of Montrose sold the estate to John Blackwood, and it remained in his family until the 1950s when it was demolished to make way for the Clober housing estate. Unlike the majority of Milngavie postcards, which were sold through various retail outlets in the town, this card was produced for the exclusive use of the occupiers of Clober House and their guests. Even as late as the 1980s a supply of these cards was still in the possession of a descendant of John Blackwood, to whom I am extremely grateful for this copy.

On The Allander

The Allander river at Jenny's Linn, 1905. James Guthrie Smith once described Milngavie as 'the child of the Allander', and many of the early industries in the town relied on it. The grain mill, and later the linen mills with their attendant bleachfields at Craigallian, Craigton and Clober, all grew up around the river. On the left of this picture a square stone pillar is just visible; this was part of the weir created to feed the Clober Bleachfields. The calico printers and the paper mill also required the clear water of the Allander, and a distillery at Tambowie was founded in 1780 because the water of the Craigton Burn was said to be of particularly good quality. The distillery closed in 1920 after a fire during the First World War.

Milngavie Golf Club was founded in 1895. On 6 May a meeting of those considered favourable to the formation of a golf club for Milngavie and district was held in the burgh hall, and interest was such that after several more meetings it was declared open for play from 8 June. It is amazing to think that in a matter of thirty-three days the proposals for a golf club could be mooted, land acquired, and holes cut (thirteen in this instance), not to mention all the other matters that would need to sorted out. Think of the red tape that exists nowadays. This *c.*1905 picture of the club house shows the corrugated iron structure that was erected in 1895 at a cost of £298 10/-, and extended in 1898 due to pressure of space. Information technology came to the club with the installation of a telephone – number 19 – in 1902, an appropriate number for a golf club house.